D1255424

THE FREUD ANNIVERSARY
LECTURE SERIES
THE NEW YORK PSYCHOANALYTIC
INSTITUTE

THE FREUD ANNIVERSARY LECTURE SERIES
The New York Psychoanalytic Institute

PSYCHOANALYSIS AND MORAL VALUES

Heinz Hartmann, M.D.

INTERNATIONAL UNIVERSITIES PRESS, INC.
New York

Copyright, 1960

The New York Psychoanalytic Institute

Library of Congress Catalog Card Number: 58-9230

Manufactured in the United States of America

This work consists of an expanded version of the lecture given at The New York Academy of Medicine on May 12, 1959.

Contents

Psychoanalysis and Moral Values

Psychoanalysis and Moral Values

The TITLE of this lecture, "Psychoanalysis and Moral Values," covers a variety of partly heterogeneous subjects. Some of them are not, strictly speaking, analytic, though they are relevant to an understanding of the evolving role of psychoanalysis in our civilization. With the others I can assume—speaking to psychoanalysts—that you will feel familiar. All these subjects have been discussed before, though not always from the points of view from which I propose to approach them today. And of some of them I feel we could say that they have been more often studied by nonanalysts than by psychoanalytic authors.

Psychoanalysis, as a psychology of the central problems of personality, is naturally in constant contact with the moral feeling and moral judgment of man. As a general psychology, it has given us the first sound explanations of the ontogenesis of moral behavior. But psycho-analysis began very early to extend its limits to cover also what we often call "applications," to cultural, religious, philosophical, artistic questions. Here, too, problems of value were constantly to be confronted. The special conditions the analyst has had to meet in these applications, the possibilities and limitations of his method of investigation, have been clearly formulated, in recent years, by Ernst Kris. Suffice it to say that even to these chapters the approach of the analyst as analyst is basically, so far as values are concerned, the same as he has become used to elsewhere in psycho-analytic psychology. His attitude is that of the psychological student of moral—or other—valuations and their interrelation with other individual or social-psychological phenomena. His objectivity is scientific objectivity, his truth is scientific truth. This attitude, however, has frequently met with misunderstanding.

Those who try to extricate from psycho-analytic knowledge directions for guiding their practical actions move—save for the exceptions to be mentioned later—on less equivocal grounds. Where the possibilities and where the limitations for such "guidance" lie we shall discuss later. Many attitudes, points of view, convictions which are commonly regarded as "analytic," are not so regarded by psychoanalysts. The picture of what is and what is not analysis fluctuates widely in the minds of men, and this is particularly true in regard to the implications as to practical action one finds, or does not find, in it. In this context I am thinking above all of the situations in which analytic considerations are allied with traditional moral, religious, social or political, or economic goals, to form an endless variety of combinations. In the construction of "Weltanschauungen," or "philosophies of life," analysis is not so much searched for the information it can give, e.g., as to the psychology of moral behavior, as for directions in practical moral questions either of the individual or of society. Some will say—in the cultural climate of our Western world today—that the analyst's opinions in such matters should carry more weight than those of others. While I do not think that such expectation is always entirely mistaken, as commonly formulated, it is wrong. We have, then, to ask ourselves, to what extent the psychoanalyst, on the basis of his psychoanalytic knowledge, can fit that social role attributed to him. One should be able to say when and in what respect such "uses" of analysis make sense, and where sense becomes nonsense. Experience tells us that there are cases in which such "use" amounts to a denial rather than a confirmation of psychoanalytic thinking. I do not propose to be systematic about these expectations. I want to discuss only one aspect that seems important in speaking to you as psychoanalysts.

I know, of course, that this trend toward basing one's way of life on analysis is very far from being general in our civilization. But it is discernible; it exists and is allied with other, parallel, and more general cultural trends. It deserves our interest, if for no other reason than because its investigation promises to shed some light on an important facet of our study of "Psychoanalysis and Moral Values."

What I say is certainly not meant to imply that I am neglecting or underrating the possible use of extratherapeutic analysis for practical purposes. It has a place also in regard to moral questions. But this is an intricate problem that we shall attempt to delineate more closely below.

Freud and Moral Values

Before attempting to elucidate these questions, we might consider what we know about the ways in which Freud approached the subjects we propose to deal with today. This aspect, "Freud and Moral Values," has never been systematically studied. We have, of course, besides Freud's works, his letters, the penetrating biography by Jones, and many memories of people still living who knew him personally. The great difficulty is to understand clearly the relationships with and the differences between various aspects of his thinking of which I want to mention a few: first his actual and "lived" moral conduct; second the moral evaluations and judgments on general problems of ethics, which he formulated as a private person; third his psychoanalytic studies of moral behavior; fourth his opinions about the necessity of moral conduct; and finally his thoughts about the possible relationships between psychoanalytic findings and theories and what in German one calls "Weltanschauungen."

To give you an example, it is not always easy to discern, in his work on the history of civilization, what derives from analytic research and what is the result of his use of psychoanalytic knowledge in developing the main themes of his personal approach to history. Freud was aware of the difference, in this respect, between these studies and the clinical and theoretical works in which he scrupulously avoided any mixing of personal positions with scientific thought. An approach to the understanding of the meaning and function of analysis by way of Freud's contributions to the history of culture—though favored by some philosophers—is actually always a detour and has often led to a distorted image of that meaning and function. It is obvious that philosophers of culture can profit from the use of psychoanalytic knowledge. However, if they turn only to Freud's work in this special, applied, field, they cannot for their own studies make the fullest possible use of the picture of man delineated by analysis.

Despite these obvious difficulties, and without prejudging the relationships between the personality of Freud and his scientific work, we should consider briefly the moral characteristics of the man whose research has contributed more than that of any other person to giving the phenomenon of morality a secure place in the natural development of the human, and has in many ways influenced the moral climate of our time.

It is very much apparent that "ethics" in the strict sense, in contrast to the psychological study of moral behavior, was not a field very close to Freud's heart. He used to quote F. T. Vischer's "What is moral is self-evident." But he had no urge to go deeper into the question of the "validity" of moral feelings or judgments. He never fully identified himself with any moral system, and even less did he attempt to develop one himself. He clearly saw the difference between true statements about facts and what one often calls "moral truth," but this question, too, was very much at the periphery of his interest. About the "necessity" of moral codes, however, he repeatedly and clearly expressed his opinion. He realized the integrative function that such codes and standards have for the individual. "Conscience" was, for him, "a necessity: [its] omission the source of severe conflicts and dangers." But, impartially, he also emphasized that in one's relations to one's fellow man "it is by no means the rule that virtue is rewarded and wickedness punished." More than once, he traced the "necessity" of moral codes to the fact that human society could not live without them. He called the superego a highly valuable possession for human society. In another connection, he showed how the development of the superego can lead to a reduction of the external means of coercion used by society. He noticed "with surprise and dismay" that "so many people obey only outer pressures," instead of developing their own moral standards. He was obviously very far from being a moral nihilist.

One clearly gets from Freud's works some indications of his moral personality. But they do not give a full picture of his moral stature. Although inferences from his scientific work on his personality as a whole, from his style of thinking on its moral aspects, are not always impossible, we know too little about these matters to make them altogether convincing. Here again we owe a debt of gratitude to those who published Freud's letters and who wrote about him from first-hand experience. From the documents available it appears that Freud had very definite and strong moral feelings, strong moral reactions to persons, to social and political events. He admired independent, autonomous morality and despised moral weakness and the tendency to compromise. Those who have pictured his moral character—Jones and other writers—lay stress on his rare courage when he found himself confronted with bitter personal criticism and disparagement, and later with long suffering and death; they emphasize the self-control and discipline that had taught him to face reality at all costs; they show his marked sense of human dignity, his independence, and his sense of duty.

His discoveries in a field that is usually thought to represent the "dark side" of human nature did not come easy to him. We know what it cost him to be objective toward those phenomena, which were untouched before by the light of science. Lou Andreas-Salome, a keen and reliable observer, said about Freud: "The results of his investigations were not at all in line with what he had wished for." One can trace in the sources available to us today how his early discoveries gradually overcame his resistances, some very marked moral resistances among them. But his uncompromising dedication to truth and objectivity, his intellectual integrity (which, of course, also implies a moral factor) allowed him to recognize what others had feared to face. His conclusions brought him finally to the realization—which restates a thought of Nietzsche's—that the highest and the lowest in man have common origins. He moved away from the otherwise widely held opinion that the genetic tracing of achievements of the mind, or of moral achievements, to instinctual origins which have not been positively, or have even been negatively, valued in themselves represents a devaluation of these achievements. He took pains to keep clinical apart from moral valuation. He was very far from being a cynic and showed no tendency for debunking.

I think one can say that Freud's system of moral values, though of course marked by his strong individuality, is not in radical opposition to the partly Greco-Roman, partly Jewish-Christian, moral traditions of Western civilization. There are close correspondences with the moral thinking of the Stoic philosophers. In clearly rejecting any and all religious creeds and systems, he did not reject the moral aspects of the Western tradition. He wished, however, that one could establish it on nonreligious grounds. Clearly, there was much in human affairs—personal, social, and cultural—that he found in need of improvement and would have liked to change. When he saw himself as a "reformer" it was mostly in close connection with what his experience had taught him about possible ways to prevent neurotic disease, and with similar questions. But when he condemned persons or institutions on moral grounds, it was hardly ever condemnation of the traditional principles but rather, in the name of these principles, a critique of actual behavior deviating from them, or of intermediate principles swerving from basic ones. How far analytic thinking, in his case as in the case of other analysts, can influence the way we measure concrete behavior against those standards is a question we shall discuss later. Of course, Freud's deepened insight into human motivation led often to applications of those moral principles on concrete behavior which differed from the current practice. But this has to be clearly distinguished from a change in basic moral principles—a point which has often been misunderstood.

At any rate, Freud, who was often surprisingly close to Nietzsche in his psychological insights, was essentially, and in contrast to him, not a "transvaluer of values"—not in the sense, that is, that he wanted to impress on his fellow men a new scale of moral values. It is a serious misinterpretation to describe him as a "teacher of morals" or a founder of a "religion." This is certainly not the way he thought of himself, nor was he *un prophète qui s'ignore*. If he thought of himself as a liberator from narrow dogmatism—and it is likely that he did—this again refers more than anything else to his insisting on the complexities of moral reality which every application of moral principles has to consider. This statement about Freud is not meant to deny that the actual impact of his work as to moral questions has been considerable, in some respects revolutionary. We shall come back to this point.

Yet, though Freud, as a person, was a man of remarkably strong moral feelings, and though his tool, psychoanalysis, indubitably has had great influence on our civilization in moral matters, his position as to any attempts—coming from inside analysis or from the outside—to deduce a "Weltanschauung" from analysis was unequivocally negative. He clearly saw that the relation of analysis to value problems was of necessity the same as that of any other science: "Psychoanalysis is not, in my opinion, in a position to create a philosophy of life" (Weltanschauung).

Practical Applications of Psychoanalysis

The step from psychoanalytic insight to its application to practical ways of dealing with human behavior has been systematically worked out mainly at one point; in the therapeutic technique (also, to a lesser degree, in mental prophylaxis and in social work). Its aim is the aim of every therapy, and the value of this therapeutic aim is not questioned; moral considerations are kept from interfering with it. This allows a minimizing of possible conflicts of valuation. The analytic therapy is a kind of technology. Most of the time the elements of this technique can be traced to the psychological insights we owe to analysis. Even so it becomes apparent that the way from science to technology is on the whole much slower and more complex in the psychological and social than in the physical sciences.

The second field in which analysis has been widely, though much less systematically, used for practical purposes is pedagogy. But here the situation, as to the problem of values, is different to begin with. In pedagogy there is no single goal accepted as unquestionably as is health in medicine. Social, moral, and other values are constantly to be considered. In the use of pedagogical techniques moral values cannot simply be put into parentheses, as they are in psychoanalytic technique. One has to face the differences in this respect between religious and nonreligious, between individualistic and conformist educational goals, between the aims of being a "good citizen" in a democratic or totalitarian society, and so on; yet there are, of course, also common elements in the ideas and practices of child rearing. For a time, the problem seemed comparatively easy. That was in the phase of analysis when one thought one could limit the aims of education to the question of prevention of neuroses. At any rate, although the aims of education do greatly vary, psychoanalytic understanding can, on principle, be immensely helpful toward the realization of many pedagogical goals.

Outside of these fields, the use of analytic knowledge, largely by nonanalysts, for practical purposes is often beset by countless difficulties and misunderstandings. It could not be otherwise. Most of these possible practical applications have been quite insufficiently studied so far by the analysts themselves. Our knowledge of the complexity of mental dynamics and of human motivation, which ought to form the basis of such applications, has come to a point at which, both in its factual and its theoretical aspects, it has become as difficult of access to most nonspecialists as are the later developments of the physical sciences. These practical applications, however, are still a challenge to the analyst. Though it could not be said that the methods have been thoroughly elaborated so far, I do not doubt that on principle analysis can be of considerable help toward the solution of social and cultural problems. Beyond these questions, we have to face the logically quite different problem I mentioned before, of the construction of "Weltanschauungen" out of the material of analysis, which is the concern of some of the many who—quite naturally in a time in which traditional value systems have lost much of their binding power—are in search of a "philosophy of life" and who try to bolster it by deriving their directions from psychoanalytic knowledge.

I hope the logical difficulties which one meets at this point shall become clearer as our investigation progresses. Here I want to say only that the answers to be found in our literature to many of the questions one could ask in this context are not always free of ambiguity. These questions have rarely been systematically studied; they are, at the same time, highly controversial. I told you what Freud had to say about attempts to base "philosophies of life" on psychoanalysis. I must also mention that there are some people, analysts as well as nonanalysts, who do not accept as valid this limitation of psychoanalysis. Now a distinction has to be introduced at this point. The case in which one uses his analytic knowledge in the service of what he recognizes to be his personal philosophy is clearly not questionable. I am thinking rather of a problem that we will meet again in a later context. I have in mind those whom one might well call "hidden preachers." They actually preach their own philosophies, their own old or new values, or old or new religions (camouflaged with analytic terminology), while pretending to teach analysis, and present what are their own "Weltanschauungen" as logically derived from analysis.

Ontogenesis of Morality

A systematic psychology of "moral behavior," including the genetic aspect, had hardly been in existence before Freud. This approach does not deal with the "essence"—whatever philosophical meaning you may give to the word— of "good" and "bad," or "virtue" and "vice," but with the attitudes, feelings, judgments, and actions that are actually viewed as morally good or bad or that determine that which is actually so viewed. The question of what one ought to consider good or bad remains outside the limits of my presentation; though I know, of course, that in the application of psychoanalytic thinking to these problems this borderline has often not been focused upon, or has not been respected. Nor will I deal with metaphysical speculations of a type that equates what we call primary instincts with a "good" and a "bad" principle; or that identifies analysis as a "principle of love," meant to oppose or reduce the power of a "principle of hate," and so on.

At least since Plato, philosophers have maintained that one has to know the "nature of man" in order to understand the problems of morality. In the light of psychoanalysis, moral valuation and moral conduct are necessary attributes of "natural man." To have firmly established this, not only in the form of *aperçus* but through painstaking and systematic observations and in the form of a well-reasoned theory, is perhaps the most important contribution Freud has made to the study of moral behavior. The rationalism of the eighteenth century, which often considered moral imperatives merely as purposeful inventions "of the priests," introduced for mainly political reasons, was wanting in psychological knowledge. Attempts at political manipulation under the guise of morality are, of course, common enough, but this explanation does not touch the point which concerns us here. Also later derivations of moral imperatives from social or economic pressures, while not completely false, were not based on sufficient insight into precisely those situations which are developmentally decisive—childhood history and the instinctual conflicts of the child. It is obvious that both religious and social forces influence moral conduct. But the factors that bring it about that man is capable of developing directions of a moral nature, ideals or imperatives which are part of his mental functioning—these factors originate in the long dependence of the human child on the adults, in the identifications and object relations that tie it to its parents, and in the conflicts that result as the consequence of the child's early sexual and aggressive development. That there exists the experience of the "ought," of a moral "good" and "bad," for the individual is essentially traceable to these beginnings. Freud's approach gives us a clear insight into the problem of moral conflict which had been puzzling to many before him, not only the conflict between morals and drives but also between morals and the ego, and the conflict between different and coexisting moral directions.

The role of the superego in the development of morals is in its outlines familiar to every analyst. Its relation, however, to moral codes and moral conduct has been stated in different ways. What I intend to say about the superego at this point will only refer to the questions under discussion today. First of all: because of its important role in the pathogenesis of neurosis, the superego has been considered by many from this angle only. I want to stress the fact that although Freud was, of course, the first fully to realize that role, he did not share in this biased view of the superego. He took a much broader view and clearly described its function in normal development, too, particularly in the development of normal moral behavior.

In the development of the superego, demands from outside are transmuted into inner imperatives—the character of a command is preserved, and the tension between demand and fulfillment. Not only the prohibitions of the parents, but also their love survives in the relation of the superego with the ego. In the course of the same development the experience arises of being responsible to oneself. What one usually calls "conscience" is defined by some as the conscious aspect of the superego. Freud considered it as one among several superego functions. He also stated that morality can be partly unconscious; and psychoanalytic investigation of moral phenomena goes beyond the limits of consciousness. The second aspect of the superego that has an immediate bearing on the evolution of moral behavior is the ego ideal—also described as a "function" of the superego by Freud. Between the two sides, we commonly find close connec-

tions as to content. This distinction between
the ego ideal and other aspects of the superego
has been seen and formulated in many philosophies of morals, as the distinction between
"the good" and the "ought and ought not"—
the imperatives. Actually, in all ethical systems
both elements are represented though in different degrees. In Greek ethics, e.g., the good
is much more in the foreground than are the
moral imperatives. Keeping this difference in
mind, it would be interesting, and feasible, to
classify the great ethical systems of mankind as
to their more narcissistic or more compulsive
character. And, still in line with this, one may
also attempt a differentiation of "goal ethics"
from "imperativistic ethics." Of course, in dealing with such questions one should not only
consider the psychology of the individual but
also the formative influences of social, economic,
and cultural processes. Every sociocultural system will foster certain types of personal morality
above others. On the other hand, there is the
contribution of the superego to the development of social and cultural tradition, which
Freud described. This contribution is related
both to the functional aspects of the superego
and to its specific contents. I mentioned before
that conflicts between the superego and the ego

(and thus guilt feeling), also contradictions between different imperatives, duties and ideals, turn out to be a necessary concomitant of human development as seen by psychoanalysis. This approach also shows clearly the vulnerability of what has been called the "moral system" of the individual. It is imperiled by the economy of the instinctual drives, in a more specific sense perhaps mostly by the aggressive drives. An imbalance may occur because, as Freud discovered, contrary to expectation, the checking of aggression can make a person's superego more tyrannical. An increase in the need for punishment beyond its habitual limits will often interfere with the integration of the "moral system," and in a variety of ways; e.g., in turning a person into a criminal. Also, if the demands of the superego become oversevere, this may lead to their inefficiency. Ontogenetically early tendencies survive in the superego to an extent that varies considerably from individual to individual. It also happens that regressive trends force individual morality on the way of sexualization, back to the object relations of the oedipal phase, out of which they originated, as in the case of moral masochism, and so on. What we have actually to deal with in judging the moral stability of a person clinically, as well as more generally, is certainly not only the genetic question. There are different degrees of reliance on the accepted codes that have to be considered; also differences as to the degree to which principles tend to be carried out in action. It is most important to evaluate the moral equilibrium as to its reversibility or nonreversibility and its vulnerability in the interplay with other factors. Practically, and theoretically, the most relevant aspect is the constancy or dependability of morality vis-à-vis reality, mostly social reality, and vis-à-vis opposing pressures from within. That is its "autonomy," which is in some ways comparable in its definition to the secondary autonomy of the ego.

A transvaluation of moral values takes place in the development of every individual. On the long way from the interiorization of parental demands after the oedipal conflicts to the more elaborate moral codes of the adult another factor becomes decisive. That is a process of generalization, of formalization, and of integration of moral values. It would be difficult to attribute what I have in mind here to the superego itself. It rather corresponds to what we know of the functions of the ego. One can say, I think, that in what one may call the moral "codes" the influence both of the superego and of the ego, particularly of the integrating and differentiating functions of the ego, are traceable. Thus we will expect to find in every system of moral values elements which directly correspond to the pressures and to the aims of the superego, and others that show the influence of the ego. It is hardly necessary to mention that these codes are incomparably more complex than the outline I can give you here.

I have to forgo a discussion of the rise and fall of moral values in the life of the individual and of society. Even after the institution of the superego the moral systems are not fully static. They are open to influences from within and without through the mediation of superego and ego; they are in constant interaction with the social structure and cultural values in which the individual lives; and their power is selectively enhanced or weakened in a process of balancing against the adaptive and integrative ego tendencies. One step in this development, best described by Piaget, takes place in the interplay of the child with children his own age. It is obvious that the efficiency of the codes will be more secure if they have strong cultural support in the environment, and, of course, one will have to consider the methods by which society manipulates individual moral development.

The elaboration of those codes during onto-genesis changes their structure, too, in that the individual learns to coordinate means and ends, and to anticipate the outcome of his actions—here again we see the active influence of ego functions. We should not forget that overlappings, superimpositions, compromises between ego interests and superego demands happen even in early childhood and continue through life. And the ego's tendency to master inner conflicts before they lead to danger threatening from outside is obvious also in the development of the superego. A considerable amount of regard for the vicissitudes of ego development, and of closeness to the demands of reality, is found, of course, in many measures of pedagogy which, besides but partly also overlapping with genuinely moral aims, try to prepare the child to average expectable reality situations.

The ego has more than one role in the establishment of the codes. What I have said so far gives a one-sided picture. Its adaptive function will often overstep its integrative capacities. Thus in an environment where there is a high premium on conformism, the ego, still as a mediator, may well enforce the neglect or the suppression of personal moral valuations, even if they have, for the individual, a considerable integrative function. In such instances, social anxiety might have proved stronger than the demands of the personal moral system. This is one of the cases in which relation to outer reality is secured at the expense of acceptance of inner reality. As an example of the opposite, of how under the pressure of superego demands, outer reality testing may be impaired, I may remind you of Freud's experience on the Acropolis.

The question of which state of balance between superego and ego regulations is the most promising from the points of view of integration, or dynamic effectiveness, or autonomy, or from the social angle can hardly be answered in a general way. I should venture the opinion that a maximum preponderance of one series of factors over the other does not represent the optimum from any of these points of view. The widely held expectation, for instance, that a maximal consideration of self-interest would provide solutions most satisfactory from all the points of view just mentioned is not borne out by psychoanalytic experience and is unlikely to prove true. If we use not these but intrinsically moral yardsticks, different states of balance may seem desirable, depending on the value systems we consider. But this topic as well as the various ways in which mankind has attempted through its history to promote certain states of equilibrium between ego and superego regulations and to impede others, I do not propose to deal with today.

Though there is, in the sense I mentioned, factual overlapping in the individual moral value systems of superego with ego functions— and though fulfillment of a superego demand may at the same time benefit self-interest, etc.— it is still necessary to distinguish as clearly as possible the factors involved. In analysis we classify the aims, the directions of mental activity, according to the three subsystems of personality whose integration we attribute to the synthetic, or organizing, function. In the past, one was handicapped in the interpretation of moral phenomena by the fact that a reasoned distinction between instinctual aims, ego interests, and moral aims was not available. Now the structural aspect of psychoanalysis—the demarcation of id, ego, and superego, introduced to account for the typical conflicts of man—allows an easier approach to those distinctions. The three types of directions we spoke of gain in concreteness and empirical fullness if they are considered in the framework of these systems. This is true of their genetic as well as of their dynamic and economic aspects. From our vantage point, the contrast of moral aims and the aims of the ego (of which the self-interests are the most widely known subgroup), or the aims of the instinctual drives, can be psychologically defined.[1] We cannot accept the interpretation of moral phenomena, as presented in various philosophical doctrines, which considers moral behavior as an explicit or implicit expression of a striving for what is useful, advantageous, or profitable. Such an interpretation is valid neither in a genetic nor in a structural sense. And this is the place to mention that in actuality moral inhibitions are very widely directed not only against the drives, but also against certain tendencies of the ego, as, e.g., against what one calls "self-interest," against "ambition," or "pride," which, in various ethical systems, are considered "evil."

It has often been emphasized that the attaining of all three types of goals we mentioned is

[1] I know that, here again, I schematize. Some ego functions can, as I said, contribute to the formation of the moral codes. Others are commonly opposed to them. The superego contributes decisive characteristics to the moral systems—we could say it is their nucleus—but not all of their features can be attributed to it.

accompanied by a feeling of satisfaction. This is true often, but not generally. The problem is more complex than it appears at first sight because of the different pleasure conditions obtaining in the mental systems (ego, id, super-ego). The three types of gratifications are, descriptively, of a very different kind. This is also one of the difficulties that besets every hedonistic philosophy. It would seem promising to attempt, for this and for other reasons, a qualitative differentiation of pleasure experiences. Such an attempt Freud has not made. It would not, however, be incompatible with his later formulations of the pleasure principle. As to the economic point of view, we could expect differences according to the prevalence of either the primary or the secondary processes; but differences more subtle than these may be involved. There is another interesting aspect to this problem. It appears that the three types of satisfaction (and this is true of different elements comprised in these types) cannot completely be substituted for one another. Instinctual gratification can often take the place of the other two types of gratification—of ego gratification and of moral or aesthetic gratification—although not fully nor under all conditions. Moral satisfaction, on the other hand, can replace even less completely, in most people, the gratification of instinctual demands. Again, this may well have something to do with the pleasure conditions prevailing in the three mental systems, and with their respective pleasure demands. But the question has not been sufficiently studied. We leave the answers to future research.

Awareness of One's Own Moral Values As Part of Psychoanalytic Insight

Moral behavior presents itself, then, as something that in early childhood has grown out of the child's relation to the objects and their authoritative demands (even "nonauthoritarian" education has some authoritarian effects, in both ways that Freud described, though, of course, in markedly differing degrees). The energies the moral demands dispose of have their origin, developmentally speaking, to a large extent outside of morality. This is not equally true of later stages. Here a factor of relative autonomy has to be considered, also in its economic aspect. In the course of development the demands are partly perpetuated, partly broadened to include others, and also, under the influence of the ego, organized. Outer laws become inner laws—this is part of the trend toward internalization which is also observable elsewhere in human development, e.g., in the function of anticipation, in the thought processes, in the danger signal. The sociocultural environment has a positive share in the establishment of moral behavior. But it is also true that relative freedom from sociocultural pressures runs parallel with the development of the superego. "Social anxiety" is transmuted into moral anxiety or guilt feeling. There are transitions between "social anxiety" and superego anxiety; for instance, the case in which demands which are not really enforced by society are still, because of inner reasons, considered by the individual as if they were.

We saw how morality becomes a part of personality, recognized as part of the inner world, despite its origins in the world outside. This seems less paradoxical if we think of parts of the ego, as for instance, "character," which we consider an essential part of it, though many of the character traits have their origin in identifications with the objects. The much-discussed question of whether morals are, because of their origins, of necessity "authoritarian" is, it seems to me, not always put in the right way. Every moral system has its origins in the relations of the child to adults who are not only loved and hated but also persons in authority.

However, the value systems evolving from these origins may have an authoritarian, a nonauthoritarian, or an antiauthoritarian character. What is common to all of them is the fact that they may appear in the form of imperatives or commands.

It is generally accepted in analysis that moral codes testify not only to the cultural environment, but also to the personality of the individual who holds them. The knowledge of his ideals and his "oughts" and "ought nots" is in normal as well as in pathological life a fruitful approach to his psychology. For the individual himself, part of his "moral system" is conscious, while another part is, as I mentioned, unconscious. But awareness can be increased. This aspect of learning to "know thyself" is often brought about by life situations. And such broadening of moral awareness occurs, often dramatically, in the course of psychoanalysis, in the form of a discovery. I am speaking of true psychological discoveries of dynamically active agents in one's own person, which are found, in analysis, to go beyond social conventions and beyond those "inventions" for the purpose of political manipulation of which I spoke before. Most men know almost nothing about the genetic aspect of their morality, and not too much about the structure and hierarchy of the values that they actually stand for in their thinking and actions. They learn about them not so much by studying ethics, but, as I just said, in real life situations and, more clearly than anywhere else, in analysis.

Certainly, one learns that many moral motivations are pretenses and excuses which serve to conceal quite different aims. That much has always been known, though less subtly, less convincingly, and less systematically. But one learns also to realize that in addition to moral pretenses there are moral motivations which have the full dynamic significance of independent forces in the mental economy. In so far as they are demands, they have the form not only of "this is demanded of me," but also of "I demand this of me." I may add here that the moral assurance that originates in the discovery of moral aims as an integral part of oneself, of being "at one with oneself" in moral action, does not necessarily include the belief in the "absolute truth" or "objectivity" of such moral aims. The assurance I have in mind stems from the recognition that these aims are one's own aims. One comes to realize that self-knowledge includes not only the recognition of one's own person as a valuating agent, but also of imperatives as one's own. In an earlier Freud lecture, Lionel Trilling emphasized that Freud's thoughts on the biological aspect of personality might well help the individual strengthen his position—a position endangered by the pressures of society in our day. If it is true that psychoanalysis helps one to realize more clearly and securely one's ideals and imperatives as integral parts of one's individual self, this may well be another contribution of analysis in the same direction. I forgo the temptation to speculate on what the actual possibilities and limitations of this contribution are likely to be on a sociocultural scale.

As we present the problem here, the recognition of acts of moral valuation, and of their imperative character as dynamically relevant, often decisive, aspects of personality, is part of self-knowledge in the same way as is the recognition of the instinctual drives and their aims in the id, and the recognition of the aims and functions of the ego. Recognition of moral imperatives both as to content and form means here their recognition as direction-giving facts; it does not necessarily mean that they are kept above the influence of, and interaction or conflict with, other mental tendencies or immune to our critical faculties. The degree to which the individual actually considers moral imperatives as obligations varies from individual to individual and is different in different cultures. In the cases in which the individual does accept some of them as fixed ends, this can be traced to the vicissitudes of his superego; it is not just due to man's devotion to an ideal of certainty as was assumed, for instance, by John Dewey.

Emanating from psychoanalysis and gradually penetrating into the awareness of many persons outside of it, we witness today some readiness to deny no longer the existence and the dynamic significance of the processes in the id. We rarely see the same degree of acceptance of what analysis has taught us about morals as an integral part of personality. With many who otherwise are ready to listen to analysis, we find rejected as "unfounded" what we know of the dynamic significance of the imperatives and ideals. I think it is clear that what I have in mind here is not just the way in which such problems occur in the analytic situation. I rather speak of the different degree to which the drive-aspect and the moral aspect have been accepted in the picture of man, as developed under the influence of psychoanalytic thinking.

Many individuals use denials or rationalizations, or both, against genuine superego commands (the word denial here covers more than its technical meaning).[2] Some use repression as Freud noted in hysterical patients and one finds this also in other cases. Denials, and especially rationalizing denials, are used by many against those elements of the codes, too, that are not immediate expressions of superego demands; these and similar defensive measures are directed against the recognition of moral demands as one's own. It often happens that individuals will behave according to their moral codes, or at any rate be continuously under their influence, and still refuse to accept that these codes are their own. They would rather try to explain their behavior in terms of their self-interests or in some other related way.

Cultural factors are often very prominent in these attitudes. Today we witness a powerful trend—but its origins are traceable through centuries—toward considering morals as an unfortunate and burdensome relic of religious or metaphysical systems. The moral imperatives of man are viewed as something that has the character of not being psychologically "real," or of being imposed and of being malignant. The misgivings felt against religious or metaphysical

2 For the adolescent such processes have been convincingly described by Anna Freud.

interpretations of morals are then displaced upon any psychological approach to morals, too, even when it has an empirical character as is the case in analysis. What one can learn from analysis on this subject is viewed by some with suspicion, and often as inconsistent with its other teachings—particularly so because analysis, which realized the role of defense and of the superego in pathology, and proved able to undo repressions, was expected to become a powerful ally in the fight to free humanity altogether from the heavy load of morality. From this point of view, such people find it easier to recognize as factual in man what has usually been called "bad" rather than what has usually been called "good." Of Freud's statement that man is not only much more immoral than he thinks but also much more moral than he knows, they would rather accept the first than the second half.

Rather intolerant of and impatient with our empirically minded endeavor to trace objectively the psychological givens of morality are those also who attempt to erect an artificial system of moral values on heterogeneous grounds. Ethical systems based on an image of man as a totally rational being are an example. That image is then used to decide what man "ought" to value. But, from our point of view, this particular picture of man is a distortion of reality. Also, analysts try to keep apart what man actually values from what, according to this or that philosophy, he ought to value. In cannot be my purpose in this lecture, to take sides for or against any ethical system. But if, for a moment, you allow me to discuss a practical aspect, that is, the potential for prevalence such systems may have, I should suggest that intellectual constructions of ethical systems which neglect the psychological forces that actually determine moral behavior are likely to impede both the stability and the power of these systems.

At this point we leave for a while our study of those processes that account for the setting and the realization of moral values. Clearly, all these reflections touch at one or the other point the theory of valuation and of values. We cannot completely avoid a discussion of such theory without leaving in the dark some relevant parts of the questions we set out to deal with today. This discussion will be of necessity brief, and incomplete.

Values, Valuation, Value Testing

We all know that the meaning of the words "value" and "valuation" varies widely, depending on the context in which the words are used (in everyday life, in economics, ethics, aesthetics, and so on). Let me take a simple nonmoral valuation: we say of a wine that it is "good." As long as this statement denotes only my experience in testing it, this is a purely empirical statement. If it means "good for," e.g., slaking my thirst, this is still an empirical statement, but here another element has already been introduced, a means-end relationship. Used by a wine merchant "good" may convey "this wine sells well." Or the word may be used quite independently of how it tastes to the subject who makes the statement, to indicate that the wine belongs to a vintage or a category of wines considered superior. In all these cases the quality of "being good" which we ascribe to the wine is in a rather simple way connected with what can be easily observed. If we use the word "good" in regard to human conduct, the situation becomes more complex. A "good deed" we call an action that agrees to some given standard —to an ideal of human behavior that we use as our model or to a moral imperative. Here we certainly do not simply make an empirical statement about an immediate experience, of the kind we did in our first example. Or, more correctly, the immediate experience is not the decisive factor in the moral value judgment. What we call "good" in judging a deed does not refer to our feeling good in observing it; it refers to its correspondence with a system of moral values. We can determine whether or not there is correspondence. We cannot decide empirically on the "validity" of the value scales we use as standards. There is a relevant difference between these standards and, for example, what one calls "standards of efficiency," which refer to a means-ends relationship. But this question, though pertinent, I do not propose to discuss in this context. As to aesthetic values, they are much closer to moral values with respect to the points under consideration here, and yet in other ways distinct from them. It seems that psychologically different types of value experience are coordinated with the different categories of values. Psychoanalysis will try to account for these differences in experience in terms of its structural and economical concepts.

Of course, what I said before is not meant to deny that one may find gratification in acting according to moral standards. Not only does every human being start by attributing goodness, in a still undifferentiated way, to objects and actions in the measure they provide satis-

faction. This linkage of satisfaction with goodness does in a way persist although the pleasure
conditions have changed and pleasure in moral
behavior has evolved and become differentiated
from that which characterizes instinctual gratification. But we learn not to attribute greater
value to what provides us with more immediate or more intense gratification. Certain pleas-
ures gradually become linked not to "good"
but to "bad." We also learn to differentiate between "morally good" according to our own
scale of values, and "morally good" according
to the scale of values of others. Generally the
distinction between "this gives me pleasure"
and "this is good" (in the sense of morals) becomes relevant for our understanding. Or to
take an example from aesthetics, "I like this
song" does not imply that I consider it a great
work of art. And it makes good sense to say,
"This symphony is great, but it is not to my
liking." To simplify the involved relationships
between pleasure and moral values, some philosophers have introduced the concept of "true
pleasure," correlated to "good deeds" or "good
men." But as this "true pleasure" already car-
ries a value accent, the attempt tends to beg the
question.

In speaking of moral values, more clearly

than in speaking of other values, there is implied a direction for action, a tendency to realize these values, rather than lesser ones, in action. This is clear in the word "imperative," but it is true also of moral values derived from the ego ideal. Our attention is drawn to the hierarchical structure of moral value systems, a structure we also find in aesthetical or intellectual values.[8] The study of values has been called a science of "preferential behavior." But I think one can meaningfully state that we prefer one object to another one though we attribute higher value to the latter. Also we apply the term preference to a much broader sector of human behavior, far beyond what is usually referred to in the term "valuation." It may well be applied to all behavior under the impact of pleasure-unpleasure balances. It may apply to the rational consideration of the means of action, even where efficiency is considered beyond the value aspect, and to aims that are profitable but not, in a stricter sense, "valued."

The expectancy of the occurrence of what is actually valued, and the means that lead to its realization, are again entirely in the field of empirical study. The question of the suitability

[8] I suppose we should leave out of our discussion the problem of "choice" which we meet here.

of the means can be approached by scientific methods.

We may ask, however, whether moral values can be called either "true" or "false," in the way statements of fact can be. Moral values may or may not agree with the code of the person who holds them, or with the prevalent codes of a given society, or with my own, the observer's code. In this there is nothing that would give us the right to apply the terms "true" or "false." What we state is only agreement or disagreement with a given code. Nor can we, strictly speaking, call any moral value an "illusion" except in the sense I shall presently discuss—though valuations may, obviously, lead to those distortions of reality we call illusions; and the application of moral value judgments may be based on illusions. I think, though, that it might be unobjectionable to distinguish in a psychological sense, in the sense of authentic expression, valuations that are genuine from those that are not. We could call moral values more authentic in this sense when, in an individual, or in a culture, they are not only represented in ideas on ethics but also are recognizable as dynamic factors in the moral aspects of a personality or a culture. There is a process of self-scrutiny with reference to what I just called the authentic quality of moral values, in regard to their authenticity in expressing the complex and more or less integrated dynamics of those factors that constitute the moral personality. I may add that in speaking of "integration" I have not a static but a dynamic equilibrium in mind. This scrutiny is, very likely, a function of the ego and it is among those activities that do contribute to the organization of action. It is part of the testing of inner reality and we might well designate it as *value testing*. The individual tests moral values against the psychological background of his acts of moral valuation. This testing is to be distinguished from assigning these values a place in any hierarchy of moral values.

Science cannot decide on what aims one "ought" to strive for, on what values should be considered supreme. Generally speaking, imperatives cannot logically be deduced from affirmative propositions. When it seems that they could, what we find is that actually some kind of imperative was hidden in the premises. We have to accept the difference between normative statements on the one hand, and descriptive and theoretical statements on the other. What is true of science in general holds good also for psychological science. Some will emphasize the dichotomy between a world of impersonal investigation of cause and effect and the world of affects, ideals, value judgments; but this dichotomy is ambiguous. The psychological processes corresponding to the latter can be, on principle, investigated scientifically. The relevant difference is rather between the empirical study of actual valuations, their study in the context of psychology or social science, on the one hand, and the decision on what "ought" to be valued, on the other. The concept of moral value has to be demarcated from the concept of those mental acts by which these values are set or realized. Psychoanalysis can decisively contribute to the study of the latter. It can contribute to our understanding of why an individual has a moral code, and why he has just this moral code, and how he succeeds, or fails, in realizing it in his actions. We still remain in the domain of empirical research if we study the question of what actual impact psychoanalysis has or can have on the moral systems of the individual in analysis, or beyond this, the moral systems of our culture. But clearly all this has nothing to do with the logical derivation of moral norms from statements of fact.

If we accept the point that "true" and "false,"

as used in science, cannot be applied to moral values, we find ourselves confronted with a current misunderstanding. It has often been said that if this view were correct, our moral codes would of necessity have the character of "arbitrariness." Actually, this does not follow, and I remind you of what I just said about "authenticity." It rather appears that a person's moral behavior is as much an essential part and a distinctive sign of his personality as is his character or his instinctual life. In this respect, at least, the setting or accepting of moral directions by an individual, or by a culture, is not to be called "arbitrary."

Freud has repeatedly been blamed, he has been accused of self-contradiction, because while trying to eliminate value judgments from scientific psychology, he still spoke with admiration and high praise of science itself. There is no doubt that he greatly valued scientific method and scientific thinking. He also thought that science could lead man to social and psychological developments which he valued and which many others, too, value. Part of this, his expectation that science may lead mankind to achieve these aims, is a proposition that can, on principle, be checked empirically; it can be validated or invalidated. That he valued the scientific method, or certain aims he thought could be reached through its application, was, of course, part of his personal value system. I should think, however, that the assumption on which the criticism is based is unwarranted—the assumption that he who tries to keep his scientific work free from the interference of value judgments should therefore renounce moral or aesthetic or cognitive valuations outside of the sphere of his scientific work.

In dealing with "moral values" in the analytic situation, there are three aspects the analyst has to keep separate. We consider, first of all, the genesis, the dynamics, the economics of the patients' imperatives and ideals, and the structure of his moral codes. Secondly we meet the problem of the confrontation of his attitudes with the codes of his family and, more generally, of the culture he lives in. There are, third, the personal moral valuations of the analyst with respect to the material presented in analysis. One cannot deny the actuality of the third factor—it is, above all, the natural outcome of the analyst's having his own value system, a "given" in the same sense as is his intellect, his interest and so on. It may, in a secondary way, get involved with countertransference. But technical knowledge will teach us that this third factor is best kept in the background in contacts with the patient; also, that in order to achieve this the analyst must be clearly aware of his own valuations and must know how to distinguish them from statements of fact. It has been doubted whether such reserve is really possible. Experience decides that it is, at least to a very considerable degree. Thus it can become part of the transference reactions of every patient that he attributes moral value judgments to the analyst which are far from being the analyst's own.

However, in the therapeutic situation something appears that we can account for only if we decide to make a distinction between the therapist's general moral codes and the one he is guided by in his therapeutic work, which could be called his "professional code." In his therapeutic work he will keep other values in abeyance and concentrate on the realization of one category of values only: health values. These are given special consideration in his work; they are taken for granted; and every therapist will, in his therapeutic work, consider their realization in his patients as his immediate and overriding concern. Is this an exception to the technical rule I just referred to, that the psychoanalyst should, in the analytic situation, try to keep his personal system of values in the background? I do not think so. It would be quite erroneous to assume that outside his professional activities the same therapist considers health values as the "highest." It is even very likely that there exists no human being for whom, in his authentic morality, health values actually do represent the highest form of values altogether. It is helpful for the analyst to keep himself aware of the difference between his general moral and his professional codes. A compartmentalization of codes in which one imperative, in our case the therapeutic imperative, takes over is not infrequent. For some, as you will know, it is evident that, so far as their work is concerned, every avenue which could lead to an increase of our knowledge deserves to be followed, regardless of the consequences. This is the professional code, or rather one of the professional codes, we find in men of science.

Quite aside from the logical point I made before, insisting on a clear demarcation of statements of fact from the question of the "validity" of values, it would be worth while to make a psychological study of the typical ways in which fact finding and valuation really interact. This is a vast field of partly unexplored possibilities. You cannot expect me to do justice, even in a superficial way, to this area of research. But two points may be pertinent here. I may mention that from morally highly valued behavior something like a reflected splendor may fall on other elements which, as we know from experience, are frequently connected with it, and we may find a similar irradiation with negative valuations. This irradiation affects what would be morally neutral if taken separately, and even what might in itself have an opposite value accent. There is a kind of contagion by positive (or negative) values of their causal, but not only causal, proximity. It is worth mentioning that this contagion actually extends far beyond the realm of the means-ends relationships. Generally, we may speak of value irradiation if elements we find to be in close contact with what is positively or negatively valued come to participate in its value accent. In this case we value in a similar way what we know to belong together in reality. According to another mechanism to which I may refer here, and which I call *value agglutination,* we expect to occur together in reality what we value in the same, or a similar way. In this case, if something is positively valued, one will tend to have other elements valued in a positive way more easily identified with it, considered part of it or in causal relation to it, than elements that have a negative value accent. This way of thinking reminds us of the primary processes and is definitely related to magical thought. But it is not found only in pathological states. In listening to, let us say, political discussions, you will have ample opportunity to discover examples of it.

As to the rather general phenomenon of value irradiation, it is often difficult to say where it can be integrated into a value system and where it leads to contradiction. If moral value irradiation extends only to causally closely related elements, the situation is comparatively transparent. But in that case, of course, the whole complex of problems centering in the questions whether or when and to what extent "ends justify means" ought to be considered. Leaving this case aside, I just want to state here that certainly, if it is applied to the data of genetic psychological studies which are of such importance in psychoanalysis, the tendency to value irradiation will often lead to contradictory valuations. Besides that tendency, and often in conflict with it, there is commonly the valuation of the genetic determinants independent of the results. And one cannot state with any degree of generality that we actually do value

[58]

the early infantile determinants taken as such in the same way that we value the later behavior patterns to which they contribute. Factors both of the kind we would value positively, and of the kind we would value negatively, go into the making of such patterns. To accept "value irradiation," beyond what it factually is, as a kind of guide to how to value those far-away determinants, would lead necessarily into confusion. There is no question of unilinear causal relationships in genetic psychology, and the same early developmental factors are very commonly at the root of both positively and negatively valued behavior. Genetic determinants, such as exhibitionism, sadism, and so on, contribute both to what is called "good" and what is called "bad" in adult behavior. The situation is rendered more complex by the "nothing but" argument, used sometimes in analysis but also outside of it. It has a theoretical meaning, but often it clearly also has the meaning of a negative evaluation. I am thinking of judgments like "This is nothing but homosexuality" or "You are a very clean person, but this means only that you really wish to be dirty." The argument has actually lost ground in analysis in recent years. As to the first meaning, its validity has been radically limited due to the development of ego psychology, which broadened our views on the hierarchy of motivations; as to the second meaning of the "nothing but" argument, one encounters it much less frequently today, probably because of a growing insight into the point I have just tried to make.

Summarizing in part what I have said in this section of my paper: psychoanalysis as a science cannot be expected to provide us with ultimate moral aims, or general moral imperatives; these cannot be deduced from its empirical findings. This is not to say that we cannot make any statements on such aims. We can judge their psychological implications. We can form a scientific opinion on what strivings they will, or will not, gratify, on their synergisms and antagonisms with other mental tendencies. But beyond this the "superiority" of one "Weltanschauung" over another one cannot be proved analytically. On the other hand, taking this for granted, psychoanalytic insight can often be used as a superior tool; it can contribute in the domain of means-ends relationships toward the realization of personal, social or cultural values. In addition, psychoanalytic understanding can powerfully contribute to the more peripheral elaborations of the basic imperatives in the moral codes, especially to their clarification and organization. I shall have some comments on this point later although I cannot possibly give you a detailed account of this area of problems today.

That there is nothing that could, strictly speaking, be called an "analytic Weltanschauung" does not imply that the analyst could or should have no Weltanschauung of his own, nor does it, of course, mean that the analyst will underrate or depreciate the directive significance of "Weltanschauungen" in the individual or in society. While the analyst learns to keep his personal values from intruding into the analytic situation, this does not generally lead to the detachment of his interest from moral concerns. Quite naturally, analysts and others acquainted with analysis will use its data and hypotheses also in their practical approach to questions of a moral, social, political, or artistic nature. What psychoanalysis can give them in this respect is increased psychological understanding, and this contribution is indeed essential. They will, in some cases at least, have a better insight into their own value systems, and their choice of means will be based on a broader knowledge of psychological factors. Yet the ultimate aims in such undertakings (neglecting at this point the contribution of instinctual grati-

[61]

fication or self-interest) are given by their personal systems of moral (and other) values. Psychoanalytic knowledge can be used, and has been used, in the service of very different "Weltanschauungen"; and the point here is that its use for different aims is not necessarily due to its being understood, or misunderstood, differently by the representatives of these aims. Nevertheless, there is a selective affinity of different "philosophies of life" with respect to the data uncovered by analysis. Some philosophies will find it easier than others to make use of the picture of man it presents. Every strictly dogmatic attitude, every taboo against psychological insight, and particularly against objective studies of instinctual matters, will limit readiness to learn from psychoanalysis. On the other hand, that humanistic philosophies seem to find it easier to integrate analytic findings with their teachings has been repeatedly stated.

Despite what I said before, it sometimes happens that a claim to greater "truth," or greater "objective validity," for a "philosophy of life" is based on the fact that it uses psychoanalytic knowledge. Ultimate moral demands are then presented as if they logically followed from empirical findings. If what I have said is correct, we will hardly be ready to grant these philosophies their claim to the prestige of empirical sciences. Some analysts may feel strongly about such systems, and may, if these correspond to their own codes, try to participate in their realization. But the analyst, even more than the nonanalyst, will be wary of claiming the authority of psychoanalysis for what he realizes to be his personal moral codes.

The question may be asked why so many tend to ignore the impossibility of deriving the validity of moral imperatives from statements of fact. Clearly, there is a strong need to give the "thou shalts" the same character of objectivity, of being accessible to proof or disproof, which we attribute to scientific statements. As long as revelation is accepted as the source of moral validity, the logical difficulty of how to derive it from facts is avoided. As to the psychological roots of the frequent incapacity to distinguish statements of fact from problems of moral validity, it seems plausible that the ways in which the primary imperatives are impressed upon the mind of the child have something to do with it. In the early years—even before internalization takes place—these demands are brought to bear on the child in a way that makes them incontrovertible and absolute. They are often presented to the child not as demands from one person to another, but as objectively valid—at a developmental stage on which the child is not capable of distinguishing this kind of "objectivity" from the one which he learns under the influence of the slowly evolving reality principle. Statements to the child such as "This tastes good" or "This tastes bad" have no such implication as long as they refer only to an expectable sensation of pleasantness or unpleasantness. But moral value judgments, too, are presented to the child in the form of statements of facts, as "This is good" or "This is bad," "You are good" or "You are bad." Here a moral imperative or prohibition is implied; it means, "Thou shalt" and "Thou shalt not." This may well be the point at which the difficulty originates of discerning between a statement of fact, which is on principle verifiable, and a moral evaluation, which is not verifiable in the same sense.

"Health Ethics" and Related Problems

In an earlier section of this paper I tried to describe the psychological characteristics and origins of actual moral ideals and imperatives. Such knowledge of the basic facts of moral life as can be gathered by psychoanalysis deserves a place in every other empirical investigation of moral phenomena. This demand is to a considerable degree fulfilled, e.g., in a brilliant study on biology and ethics by J. Huxley which is probably familiar to many of you (however, the conclusions this author draws are at some points at variance with our own). Many attempts have been made to account for morality from the viewpoints of biology, sociology, or culturology. They help us to understand certain functions of morality, the development of specific ethical systems, the contributions they may make toward the solution of social, cultural or biological problems; what their prospects are in a given environment, whether they are in line with certain historical trends or the trends of evolution, and so on. To discuss them here would mean to go far beyond the limits I have set to this lecture. Yet I must mention at this point that some of these attempts tend intentionally or unintentionally to transgress the boundaries of empirical science by making factors that had been introduced for the purpose of explanation serve at the same time as yardsticks of value, to which is then attributed some degree of "objectivity." Then the direction of biological or historical evolution, often with the help of an ambiguous concept of progress, is used as a criterion of moral behavior. Obviously, also other attempts to achieve "objectivity" of moral principles by basing them on heterogeneous grounds—let us say by correlating their validity with the contribution to "happiness" they are supposed to make—will be questionable in this respect.

One can, on principle, verify whether moral behavior of a certain kind is biologically useful; whether it has or has not survival value for the individual or for society (but, considering what we know about the genesis of moral valuations, it would be absurd to expect that only what has survival value for individual or species would actually be called "good," or that everything called "evil" must have the opposite effect); whether it is social or antisocial; whether or not it contributes to happiness. It is, however, particularly difficult to determine in how far "good" contributes to happiness—happiness being a highly complex psychological phenomenon, and the concept being ambiguous. At any rate, in all these cases the appointment of happiness, or biological advantage, or any utilitarian aim, as a supreme moral value is still the expression of an empirically subjective attitude. It cannot be deduced from any data of biology, or of social science, or of any other science. I hope you won't take this to mean that I think one "ought not" to strive for those aims.

My point is rather that in the cases I have in mind, empirically subjective values are posited as if they were "objective" and accessible to empirical validation. Others clearly avoid this error and openly proclaim such directions as their ultimate "aims," as their "programs," their "ideologies," which they try to realize as best as they can—without presenting their "validity" as derived from statements of facts. To discuss social or political ideologies is clearly beyond the reach of this paper, nor can we touch the interesting problem how, in the course of historic development, such aims can become part of moral codes. Still, we may mention that in appraising their prospective power one will, of course, have to evaluate, among other factors, the support they may expect to find from those psychological tendencies that determine human behavior. We have to admit that so far we have quite insufficient knowledge of the psychological synergisms and antagonisms between such tendencies and, for instance, strictly moral directions. But this has led us far afield.

There is only one other approach to the problems of moral values, an approach somewhat similar to those just mentioned though usually not based on any specific and explicit philosophical system, that I wish to discuss at this point. It is the broad overlapping of health values and moral values, very characteristic of the thinking of many today. As some of you may remember, I have written elsewhere about misuses of the concept of health and more recently Reider has added to that critique. Psychoanalysis has taught us to view the phenomena of mental health and mental disease in the context of psychological processes whose importance for their understanding had previously not been realized. Some relationships between moral factors and health and disease can be clarified. That current trend thus deserves our attention. It soon appears, however, that instead of studying the connections between moral phenomena and the phenomenon of health, the followers of this trend tend to discard altogether the psychological peculiarities of moral feelings or judgments; and, incidentally, they often tend also to forget the significant difference for society between mental health and moral behavior. The functions which morality has in society—and by which it is often justified—cannot possibly be fulfilled by "health." And, by the way, not everything that is considered "bad" in a social value system, because it is considered harmful to a given society, can be traced to neurosis. Such a lack of discrimination is confusing. It is quite as confusing as it would be to let moralizing intrude into our assessment of clinical states.

Mental health cannot be defined without reference to processes of integration, and we have emphasized before the integrative function of moral codes. Thus a certain lack of clarity in distinguishing the sphere of "health" from the sphere of "morals" may be understandable —though it could be avoided because, in analysis, we differentiate several forms and levels of integration. Also, we know empirically that the correlations between morality and sanity are complex and in many of their aspects not sufficiently studied. If we continue, as we have done throughout this lecture, to consider only the empirical question of what is actually valued (and not the nonempirical question of what one "ought" to value), it is obvious that there are many neurotics who are "highly moral" and many, sometimes the same ones, who are socially useful, while there are many "healthy" people who are neither the one nor the other—contrary to the expectations of the representatives of a health ethics.

What I call *health ethics* here tends to simplify those correlations. In addition, it tends to substitute health values for moral values—

which is a different proposition again. This is often formulated as "There are not moral or immoral people, three are only healthy and sick people." "Health" is considered a valid moral criterion. What I have just described is seen rather regularly, because of the nature of the analytic situation, as a transient phenomenon with our patients, and I will have a few words on this later. But, as I said, this attitude extends far beyond the number of analytic patients or analyzed persons. The equation of mental health values with moral values may come to mean an equation also of moral "badness" with mental dysfunction. This aspect, though commonly considered to be an advance in tolerance, be-trays a relation to pre-Freudian thinking. At the start of his studies in neurosis, Freud had to state emphatically that neurotics should not be considered morally inferior to so-called nor-mal human beings. As a matter of fact, "health ethics" can be as "moralistic" as any other type of ethics. The strictness and rigidity which are so often found in moral demands are displaced onto another field. Some wishful thinking, too, may well have a part in this form of "ethics": the hope that in attacking neurosis individual therapy can do away also with everything that is considered "bad" in human nature. The problem seems so much less serious if instead of facing the unpleasant reality we speak of "neurotic traits." For that pseudo-ethical approach the authority of psychoanalysis is not infrequently claimed, but it is actually the outcome of many parallel trends in our civilization. From what I have said and what I will say, it will be clear that while it is true that followers of this trend often adopt analytic knowledge, the trend does not coincide with the analytic approach to these problems. Psychoanalysis tries whenever feasible to look through rationalizations and to penetrate to the true motivational dynamics hidden behind them. In contrast to this, we see in the trend under discussion, analytic knowledge—often half-knowledge—put in the service of rationalization, and I remind you here of what I said on this kind of rationalization in the first part of this paper.

Even with the propounders of "health ethics," health valuations do not actually have the psychological character of moral imperatives. There is, then, a psychological misstatement implied in the conception: the substitution for genuine moral valuations of valuations of a different kind. Conflicts between moral and other valuations can, as I said before, be found in every human being. But the substitution of one category for another, psychologically different one, creates conceptual confusion. A disadvantage in the practical handling of those conceptions is also found in their extreme arbitrariness. Many concepts that make perfectly good sense clinically, like narcissism, aggression, passivity, and so on, have to be considerably distorted in order to be used, as they often are, for the purpose of moral evaluation. Thus, to give a trivial example, aggression may in this context easily be made to appear "good" by relating it to elements that are charged with health meanings, such as vitality, strength, lack of neurotic inhibitions, or by implying that the opposite attitude would be a sign of masochism. But it is equally easy to devalue aggression by referring to its opposition to libido and thus characterizing it as something "contrary to life." The function of frustration tolerance will easily be devalued as "masochism" and so forth. Everywhere, "health ethics" is related to both the "value irradiation" and "value agglutination" which I discussed before. Moral values irradiate health values and vice versa; and the expectation is created that these two will be mostly found together in reality.

All this is also connected with what I said in the beginning of this lecture. If we do not recognize, if we deny in ourselves, the psychological nature of moral valuation, not only distortions of our authentic codes and directions will result, but also the picture of the reality we evaluate will be often distorted—in our case the picture of what we empirically know about the characteristics of what we call healthy and sick. Thus objective insight into both inner and outer reality might be affected as a consequence of this departmental confusion. For obvious reasons, the situation becomes even less clear where moral evaluations of social or cultural systems are expressed in terms of "healthy" and "sick." You will understand that I do not question that "health" is a value although I do not discuss here its position in the hierarchy of values. What I suggest is rather that we should study the actual relationships between what is called "healthy" and what is called "moral" and that we should avoid the confusion that results from a substitution of one for the other.

What I said about "health ethics" is to some extent true also of the frequent abuse of the concept of maturity. Health and maturity are, indeed, often used as nearly synonymous. The concept of maturity is, of course, meaningful in a specific sense in psychology, as it is in biology. However, the frequent occurrence of the term in common usage, and its uncritical fusion with basically heterogeneous concepts, tends to cover up the very interesting empirical problems we see here rather than to clarify them— I am thinking of the actual correlations of maturity and health, of maturity and moral conduct, etc.

Still speaking of attempts to substitute other values for moral values, I should like to append here a brief note on a special instance. Though such an occurrence is not as wide spread as those discussed before, it has the advantage that we can closely observe it in the analytic situation itself. Many patients go through a phase in analysis in which the technical rules that govern the psychoanalytic process are considered, by the patients, as a kind of moral code, as a model for behavior outside analysis, or they are even broadened into a kind of "Weltanschauung." This we understand as a transference phenomenon, as the result of an identification with the analyst, of the analyst temporarily taking the place of the superego or of those objects the relations to which have been at the origin of superego formation. The analyst's insistence that the patient adhere to certain rules of a technical nature may become a moral demand for the patient. Deep interpretation, the broad range of communication, un-limited self-revelation, widest permissiveness, the discarding of every consideration which stands in the way of full psychological under-standing, as practiced in analysis—all these are then regarded as the only "right" ways to deal with interpersonal problems outside of analy-sis too. The avoidance of what we consider moral value judgments, characteristic of the analyst's attitude toward the patient, is taken as a model by the patient who tries, then, to avoid moral value judgments in his own deal-ings with other people. All this we theoretically expect to come to an end with the termination of a successful analysis. But with some patients it does not. Also, one might well speculate on why, in our culture, many other people who have not been in analysis themselves find it so easy to adopt these technical codes in the place of moral principles.

"Self-Interest" and "Rationality"

And now some brief comments on two points which certainly deserve a fuller treatment than I am able to give them today. Still in line with what I said before, and in the same context, I shall speak first on the position attributed by many to those ego functions commonly designated as "self-interest." Earlier in this lecture I referred to the typical conflicts between the pursuit of self-interest and moral demands. This conflict is, of course, everlasting and so is the frequent outcome in victory for the former. But this is not, now, our immediate concern. Here I just want to accent the fact that such an outcome is often valued in a special sense and that this valuation is sometimes presented as being derived from psychoanalytic knowledge. It seems to many an obvious conclusion from thoughts which are central in analytic psychology. Acting according to self-interest is, then, considered more "healthy," more "rational"—in a general way more "legitimate"—than acting according to moral principles. It is presented as the result of having conquered successfully the archaic taboos of earlier days, as an indication of individual or cultural progress on which one may pride oneself. Again, I do not suggest discussing our personal evaluation of these ideas, and I repeat that psychoanalysis as such is "not in a position" to decide questions of that kind. However, I may say a few words about the psychological tenets, supposedly analytic, to which these statements, where they are explicit, do refer. There is the view, not infrequently underlying them, that in psychoanalysis moral imperatives and ideals are considered as less psychologically "real" than are other mental tendencies; that they are, in some way or other, considered as "illusions"; or that an individual is considered the more healthy, the more he has freed himself from the directions set by his moral codes. That these are distortions of analytic teachings has been said in the first part of this paper and I do not need to revert to the subject. But a remark on the implications of those ideas as to "health" may be to the point. It is true that neuroses often make it impossible for an individual to pursue what he considers to be in his best self-interest. If so, a successful analysis will remove this impingement of neurosis on these ego functions—the same way as it does with impairments of other ego functions. But this hardly warrants the assumption that according to the analytic view the dominance of this special group of ego tendencies is a prerequisite of health and that to subordinate other tendencies to what is "useful" is characteristic of healthy as against neurotic behavior. Actually analysis has contributed much to shattering the widely held opinion that the only decisive motivating power in man is self-interest. And even apart from the analytic emphasis on the motivating powers of the id and the superego, in the ego itself those tendencies are only one group of functions beside others. Nor do the strivings toward what is "useful" represent, psychologically speaking, a homogeneous group. There cannot be such a simple correlation with our concept of health. The prevalence of these tendencies does not reliably indicate whether or not the conflicts with the drives have been successfully dealt with, whether the superego demands have been harmoniously integrated, etc.

Action in the service of self-interest has often been termed "rational"—wrongly, as we shall presently see. What do we actually mean when, in analysis, we speak of rationality? It should mean logically correct thinking and the consideration of available (outer and inner) data; also the checking on these facts and their connections according to certain commonly accepted rules. Where the objects are the irrational aspects of the human mind, rationality, according to this definition, clearly means that we should not avoid them or deny their factual existence, as certain forms of "rationalism" have done, but that we should consider them fully, in thinking and action. As to action, we can say that "an individual that is directing his behavior according to the ends, means, and subsidiary consequences, and in doing so rationally balances the ends against the means, the means against the subsidiary consequences, and finally the various possible ends against each other" (Max Weber) acts in a purposively rational way. "Rational," in this sense, designates a psychologically specific approach to outer and inner reality, and in this approach resides the overwhelming significance of rationality. On the basis of our purely psychological definition of rationality in cognition and action, nothing can be termed "rational" that is considered an "ultimate end." Goals can be considered as rational only if they are viewed as partial goals in a broader means-ends complex. Ultimate ends, then, are considered as psychological givens; the ways to approach them, however, can be described as to their degrees of rationality. This means also that rational action can be used in the service of both morally positively and morally negatively valued aims. And it is often true that a deed, negatively valued from the point of view of morals, but arrived at by means of rational calculation, is even more severely condemned than if it were the outcome of emotional action.

Psychoanalytic usage, though, is not always limited to these meanings of "rational" which recommend themselves by being unambiguous psychologically. Freud is not quite consistent in the use of the term. Occasionally he uses intellect, scientific spirit, reason as synonyms. There is also a passage in his *New Introductory Lectures* where he states that "the very nature of reason is a guarantee that it would not fail to concede to human emotions and to all that is determined by them, the position to which they are entitled." Such a function of reason would certainly go beyond what we have called "rational" before, but it can still be accounted for in strictly psychological terms: it refers to what is called, in analysis, the synthetic or the organizing function of the ego. But "reason" and "reasonable" with Freud and with others often imply a set of explicit or implicit value judgments. Such concepts, however, cannot any longer be defined in terms of empirical psychology. They mean something different in the framework of different value systems. In extreme cases, the statement that behavior is "reasonable" may only mean that it is legitimate according to certain codes. Now, we might well agree to the valuation of reason in one or the other meanings in which the word is used. But this is not our point here. We must try to state what is definable in terms of empirical psychology, especially if we want, as I do here, to mark more clearly the reach of psychoanalysis as a science with respect to these problems. In using the word "reason" in scientific and particularly in psychological discourse, one should be aware of this ambiguity. You know, of course, that many great thinkers have attempted to base ethics on "reason," and I suppose that the personal philosophies of some of you follow their lead at least to some extent. But I think you will agree, that the philosophers of reason, at least those among them who are at all interested in linking this concept with concrete mental functions, could profit by carefully studying the vast area of empirical findings on rational and irrational behavior which we owe to psychoanalysis.

Degrees of Generality of Moral Demands

If we consider moral values, imperatives, ideals, as we do here, solely as to the processes that went into their making and as to the interaction of valuations with other mental processes (and, of course, their relations with sociocultural factors), our approach is certain to be called "relativistic." This is in one sense correct; that is, in so far as in this approach no place is reserved for an "absolute" or "objec-

tive" validity of these values. It is not correct,
and I mentioned this before, if one takes it to
mean that the setting of, and feeling bound to,
moral values is "arbitrary." I have explicitly
discussed the origin and actual binding power
of our own codes. The adoption by or imposi-
tion on the adult of value systems, important
as they may be for individual and society, will
always depend for their dynamic impact on the
psychological backing they do, or do not, find
in the individual's mental history. I hope I have
formulated this carefully enough to avoid any
inference that the codes an individual adheres
to would exhaust, if I may say so, his moral
possibilities. Every individual, and every culture, owns a moral potential as a psychological
given, not all aspects of which are necessarily
realized in the actual moral systems. It is clear
enough that changes in such codes do occur—
but not every accrual to, or obsolence of, or,
generally, change in the codes has equal dynamic possibilities; not every code can be made
"one's own" to the same extent in the sense
defined before.

There is a strict form of "relativism" that
tends to underrate the common elements shared
by different moral systems. What is the truth
in this matter? About the extent of their varia-

tions, we owe decisive insights to anthropology. The common elements did not escape the attention of most anthropologists, nor, for that matter, of many observers in other fields. For this I shall quote here only two instances. According to Kluckhohn, murder, unlimited lying and stealing are everywhere valued negatively; also something like a principle of "reciprocity" is recognized everywhere. Montagu states that murder is generally considered a crime; some incest regulations are universal; nowhere is cannibalism regular practice. Also, the duty of the adults to take care of the children is generally accepted; a certain respect for private property is, too, and so is respect for the dead of one's own group. The analyst will be ready to accept, he will indeed expect, that there are such commonalities. There are elements common to all men as to the situation in which their young develop, as to the structure of their mental apparatus, as to its growth and development, more specifically as to superego formation and so on. These phenomena naturally result in common elements in moral valuations also. It is easy to see, though, that they do not result in one ethical system common to all. We will not go into detail as to whether any definite trends in this respect are traceable in the history

[83]

of mankind. Freud, who leaned heavily on an evolutional approach to anthropology, thought that there were. To give one example: for him the growing internalization of aggression in the formation of the superego was a main trend in the development of civilization. A trend toward growing ego autonomy, which we believe to be manifest in the development of at least some civilizations, may play a role, too, in the ways moral codes are formed. But the problems that confront us here point far beyond the scope of this lecture.

Effects of Psychoanalysis on Moral Systems and Moral Judgment of Others

Would it be possible to say that people who have undergone an analysis have a uniform hierarchy of moral values, or at least very similar moral codes—perhaps what Plato expected of the sages? Experience does not unequivocally decide in favor of this expectation. There are some similarities which we will discuss later; but we cannot deny that even among psychoanalysts who have not only undergone analysis but in their therapeutic activities follow more or less the same professional code, we find representatives of different "Weltanschauungen" and corresponding differences in their general moral codes. It is evident that individual differences are not obliterated by analysis and that this is not less true of the moral aspect of personality than of its other aspects.

In denying that moral imperatives can legitimately be derived from psychoanalytic findings, it might appear that I limit radically the possible effects of analysis on moral life. I think that our conclusions are unavoidable, if we are unambiguously ready to accept analysis as what it clearly is; that is, if we abandon any attempts to project our philosophies of life onto it. But these conclusions refer only to one aspect of our problem. It is also true that given a set of ultimate aims, analysis has a significant potential for clarifying and organizing them, and, under certain circumstances, also for helping toward their realization.

We have not touched so far on the question of what are the empirically demonstrable effects of analysis on moral behavior. This is the area to which I propose to turn at this point. We should not be surprised to find that the often far-reaching changes of personality analysis can effect may have an influence also on its moral aspects. There is a continuum from true structural changes resulting in modifications of moral behavior to those more superficial alterations which affect only the intellectual ideas about ethics. The effects of analysis, which are brought about in the analytic situation, we may call intensive; we may call its effects extensive if we think of all those manifold ways in which analysis has penetrated into common knowledge. In considering the latter we will remind ourselves that not everything that is often considered as "analytic influence" has its real or sole origin in psychoanalysis. There are cultural trends which, without having their source in analysis, run parallel to it in some of their effects. The line of demarcation is not always easy to trace. Generally, in the field of analytic influence on moral behavior our knowledge is scarce and what we know has never been systematically stated. What I can tell you about it does not go beyond some impressions and some tentative and rather sketchy formulations.

Some of the factors inherent in analysis create the conditions for moral change, and affect only indirectly the moral aspects of personality. It has often, and rightly, been stated that analysis frequently enhances man's capacity to realize more fully his potentialities. If moral inadequacy is due to neurotic causes, successful analysis can remedy it. The more successful integration psychoanalysis commonly promotes may have effects also on moral conduct. Certain moral inefficiencies, due to a lack of communication between the superego and the ego, may in this way be mitigated. The broadening of self-awareness, which is, of course, a regular result of analysis, can influence the degree of consistency of the "moral systems," etc. But here experience suggests a note of caution, if we wish to come to an objective evaluation. While we have enough empirical evidence to support these statements, it would be quite unwarranted to assume that such are always the results, even of successful analyses.

Analysis is as little a never-failing key to morality as it is, as Freud was the first to realize, a reliable key to happiness. I remind you again that for us, analysis is primarily a therapeutic and not a moral instrument. Also, for us neurosis is not, as it is for some others, primarily a "moral problem." Obviously we try to relieve a patient of his neurotic suffering, even if there is no chance that in the process he will also become a morally better person, judged by his codes or by those of society. Here as in many other respects Freud cautioned against unwarranted optimism: "Why should analysed people be altogether better than others? Analysis makes for unity but not necessarily for goodness." This is no doubt true; it does not imply, however, that there are no individuals whom analysis can help to approach this state. But, of course, we will not forget that moral changes induced by psychoanalysis may be differently valued in the framework of different value systems.

I said before that people who have been analyzed, or those who have otherwise been under the influence of analysis, have not necessarily the same moral codes, but that we still find commonalities in some respects. One, the clearest one, is their moral attitude toward sexuality and, beyond this, to functions of the body in general; though even here one sometimes meets exceptions. The change to a more relaxed attitude toward the sexual behavior of both adults and children is, by the way, one of those cases I thought of in speaking of developments partly but not wholly due to analysis; other historical factors clearly participate in this trend. The change in attitude toward aggression is different—less clear and less general. Whatever other factors may cause this difference, it seems plausible that the social aspect of morality plays a role in it. Full discharge of the sexual drives is rarely as damaging to society as one has assumed in the past; the same cannot be said of the full discharge of aggression.

Another attitude, rather commonly shared by both these groups, is the high value placed on the facing and acceptance of outer and inner reality, on intellectual integrity, and on self-knowledge. Although it has been sometimes so misconstrued, "acceptance" of reality does not imply, in the context of analytic thinking, passive submission to a given social system. Self-knowledge also has moral implications, to which we shall turn later. But I want to mention here that the valuation of the "know thyself" is to be found in many otherwise different value systems —and not only in the best known, the Socratic philosophy. It has been a widely accepted imperative from the Delphic Apollo to Freud. This is but one instance of an interesting phenomenon: the convergence of some actual effects of analysis with the demands of certain philosophical and religious doctrines.

Speaking to an audience of analysts, it seems hardly necessary to emphasize that, in the process of analysis, the dealing with an individual's moral system takes place on many levels at the same time. His moral feelings, judgments, actions are not considered in isolation but in their relatedness to the total personality of the patient. Their psychological background is being scrutinized, beyond the reach of conscious

[89]

motivation and the conscious aspects of moral conscience. Part of this process is the analysis of the superego, but it actually includes also the superego's relations to the other mental institutions and to reality.

Only in the analytic situation, and not through other contacts with analysis, are deep modifications in the economy and distribution of a person's feelings of guilt commonly brought about. To counteract a frequent misunderstanding: we do not expect an analyzed person to have no guilt feelings (we consider the capacity to experience guilt an entirely normal characteristic of human experience). But we expect that his guilt reactions will be more clearly in line with the integrated parts of his personality, with his authentic moral codes, and with the reality situations. "In the ideal case," Nunberg writes, ". . . the superego becomes more tolerant." This is no doubt true; tolerance here refers to a higher degree of integration with the ego. Superego directives will also often be approved and taken over by the ego. This, together with the changes in the economy of aggression accompanying it, is certainly one of the main avenues to a change of moral behavior through analysis. I think it is also true that a more tolerant superego may sometimes mean a greater consistency in the application of the moral codes, and even give them a stronger dynamic impact on behavior. It is, however, difficult to state in a general way which degree of tension between superego and ego is most propitious from the point of view of moral conduct—or, by the way, from the point of view of health. That normalcy does not imply an abolition of this tension, I have said before.

But let us return to the factor of self-knowledge, so intimately connected with the process of analysis. At this point I will not discuss, as I did before, the valuation of self-knowledge but rather its impact on the processes of moral valuation. Despite what the great Plato thought about it, we do not believe in a simple correlation between the steps toward insight and the steps to moral improvement. A remark of Freud's is to the point here. It is from the same letter from which I quoted before: "I do not agree with Socrates and Putnam that all our faults arise from confusion and ignorance." Still, we cannot write off the cases in which increased self-awareness does have an effect on the moral codes. Broadening of self-knowledge, including also motivations which are commonly unconscious, can lead to a broadening also of the sense of responsibility, the avoidance of easy rationalizations, and so on. Furthermore, it seems likely that a clearer and more objective awareness of motivation and of one's actual value structures also allows a more subtle form of control, which is certainly one of the factors with which we are concerned in considering moral conduct.

The recognition of one's authentic values, and their distinction from those which are not authentic, is not infrequently sharpened in the course of the analytic process. This will not change a "bad" person into a "good" person, or only rarely. What it means is that the codes can become less distorted, often less one-sided, expressions of the moral aspect of personality. The individual can learn to see more clearly the moral aims, ideals, imperatives he actually adheres to and to understand them in the context of his personality, and as his own. You know how carefully we avoid, in analysis, imposing ethical demands on our patients. But what often does happen as a consequence of analysis is that the patient's own authentic moral values become dominant in his codes.

On the other hand, it may also occasionally happen that contact with what analysis reveals about human motivation may lead certain personality types to a devaluation of moral values.

[92]

Although this may occur in analysis, in a successful analysis it tends to be a transitional phase only. What I have in mind here is the effect of that "genetic mistake" I mentioned before: noticing that highly valued moral behavior has roots in mental tendencies which are not so, or even oppositely, valued, leads some individuals to the conclusion that the high valuation had been an illusion. This may lead to the rejection of analysis because of its alleged capacity, or even tendency, to destroy values. The popular picture of the psychoanalyst as a cynical debunker has its origin here. I think, however, that the feeling of disenchantment, of life being valueless and meaningless, which we so often encounter today, is comparatively rare in analyzed persons. What one commonly calls the "meaning of life" has to be defined psychologically in terms of man's attitudes toward life. The discovery of inner reality in analysis does change these attitudes and may change the meaning life has for the individual. A broadened insight into human motivations may well make certain "meanings of life" unacceptable. But one should not forget that, on the other hand, clear consciousness and a higher level of organization of one's self are for many among the strongest factors that

[93]

give "meaning." The process of analysis does not point in the direction of nihilism.

In analysis, man is confronted with a more encompassing reach of "his good" and "his bad" than he had been aware of before. To a lesser extent, analytic knowledge acquired outside analysis can work in the same direction. The confrontation with the unconscious mind, the undoing of the blind spots, as to the "good" as well as the "evil," can give to moral awareness a depth dimension that it would be lacking otherwise. Though approaching the problem on the basis of quite different postulates and, in the main, with different intent, and using different tools, all great religions, too, have aimed at this confrontation. Obviously there is a tendency easily recognizable in some civilizations (coexisting in our own with an opposite trend which we discussed before) which would deny not only in oneself but also in mankind what would be deemed "radically bad." Thus with many persons for whom the idea of God persists, the idea of the devil has vanished. Whatever the reasons for this development, the result has been a degree of optimism concerning the nature of man against which Freud has often warned—and which many of us, too, would judge ill-considered.

[94]

I spoke of the broadened vista on moral phenomena which is owed to analysis; and of how it leads, among others, to a fuller recognition of ideals and imperatives as psychologically real aspects of our inner world. With some it leads to a more lucid and more substantiated realization as to which of these are basic and which are derivatives, or, rather, to a better understanding, at least in regard to one's own person, of that hierarchical structure which is a characteristic element of all systems of valuation. And contradictions in the moral codes can be eliminated—this elimination often being an indication of the strengthening of the ego—though it would be hard to find a personal moral system which is really free of contradictions. Referring to the well-known experience of finding contradictions not only in the moral value systems, but also between moral values and others, such as health values, aesthetic values, intellectual values, social values that are not in themselves moral, I may add that here analytic self-insight can render the same service, not in the sense of any so-called "objective" order of values, but with reference to personal and actual orders of valuation.

To say that it is a long way from the clarification of ethical principles to moral conduct is to state the obvious. But I should think that a clear and systematic awareness of actual moral motivations could affect moral action, too. Furthermore, a truer insight into the inner implications of an action will often lead to a regrouping of motivations—even without a change in the balance between a person's moral and other motivations having taken place. The point is that even without any surrender, or alteration, of the moral codes, this deeper insight will often of necessity lead to changes in the field of their application to moral action. Again, you may say, that all this would not, in itself, turn what we would call an immoral into what we would call a moral person. To this anticipated argument I fully agree. But wouldn't you concede that given a certain set of genuine imperatives and ideals, with a certain degree of dynamic power, the impact on moral conduct would likely be more clearly delineated and less vulnerable to rationalizations than it would be without that work of scrutiny that analysis makes possible? This too we can describe as contributing toward greater consistency, this time in regard to conduct; you remember that earlier we described the factor of greater consistency in regard to the moral value systems. Consistency in this sense is often considered an imperative; and, even where it is not, it is certainly an essential aspect of morality.

It is hard to state with any degree of certainty or generality how far analysis, or analytic knowledge, can be used in applying moral standards to the moral evaluation of others. No doubt, one would call "just" only that evaluation which is based on psychological knowledge—of an action, or a person. Today, one would hardly call an action "good" or "bad," without including its motives in one's evaluation. This point is clearest in the ethics of "good will." But analysis tends to go beyond this in considering moral conduct. Some will, of course, state by definition that only "good will" should be called moral, in the strict sense of the word. But while we certainly do not think that this kind of motivation must always be a "rationalization," it may well be rationalization, and the distinction is not always easy. And certainly in order to grasp the autonomy of moral conduct, its consistency, its reliability—factors we discussed before—we need a deeper knowledge of a person's genuine imperatives and ideals in their interaction with other motivations. Can this be achieved? I think it can; in some analyses. On principle, then, we possess in the analytic process a method for ascertaining a person's moral system in a fairer and more subtle way than is accessible to other methods; but this way is, alas, severely limited in its range.

We meet serious difficulties if we try to use on interpersonal relations outside of it the cues and the checks which have proved their value in applying the psychoanalytic method in the analytic situation. Outside, the cues are frequently not available and the checks are mostly not applicable. Still, this stricture is not absolute. Psychoanalytic psychology can often be used to considerable advantage beyond the analytic situation in order to determine how far moral actions and motivations are genuine and how far they correspond to a given standard. Of course, in these cases our judgment on the psychological background of the actions can sometimes be a matter of guesswork only. But one should not forget that this is no less true of any other approach to these problems. And it is likely that in these matters the analytically informed guess will prove more often correct than the common-sense guess. It will consider many more variables than a nonanalytic approach would consider. But the analytically informed judgment will often be not only more complex, but also more subtle. A comprehensive study, on these grounds, of moral casuistry (in the original sense of the word) does not exist. It might be instructive to attempt it.

There is no doubt that in our time the spreading of analytic insight has had an influence not only on the moral codes, which we discussed earlier, but also on the demand to base moral evaluations on more complete psychological knowledge. Such a trend, at least in its beginnings, may well have a restricting effect on the assurance with which the moral actions, or the moral personality, of our fellow men are evaluated. Expectations that "only this kind of a person would perform this good deed," and "only that other kind this bad deed" are mostly conventionalized and widely hallowed by tradition. Such preconceived correlations save one the labors of psychological investigation. But when checked against our experience, they often prove wrong. Thus every broadening of psychological knowledge represents in this field, too, a break with our habits of thinking, often with the customary value expectations of our cultural environment also. The traditional order, or rather the traditional coordination of moral valuation and psychological understanding, falls apart and it takes some time until the equilibrium between one's knowledge and one's concrete valuations of behavior is re-established and their correlation becomes again "natural," that is, detached from the scientific atmosphere and made part of everyday life. The trend toward a more comprehensive and less biased view of this field is noticeable today—and so is the concomitant confusion. But there is no reason to doubt that it will give way to a regained integration, on a higher level of insight into human motivation, and that psychoanalysis will have considerable influence on this process.

Summary

I have tried in this lecture to define psychoanalysis in its relations to problems of morality. I first gave you a brief outline of its contributions to the understanding of the phenomena we call "moral," of their contents and of their forms, and of their interrelations with other aspects of personality. This led to an attempt to delineate what this knowledge, as self-knowledge, can mean in terms of our attitudes toward our own moral imperatives and ideals. A look at the meanings of the concept of value guided us to the conclusion that analysis cannot, by itself, provide us with the ultimate ends for the moral aspects of personal, social, or political behavior. But we also pointed to those contributions toward clarification and organization, in the framework of a given system of valuations, or, more specifically in the framework of given moral codes, which can be gained simply and directly from psychoanalytic knowledge. I regret that I could not be more specific on the important and interesting question how this knowledge could bear fruit in its confrontation with old and new "philosophies of life." I finally gave you some general indications of the extent of the actual effect, on different levels, of the psychoanalytic process and of psychoanalytic knowledge on moral systems, on moral behavior, and on the moral judgments we pass on others.

This lecture was addressed to you above all as psychoanalysts; the selection of the points I made and certain features of my presentation would probably be different if I were to address another audience on the subject. It is true that some of the questions I raised are not what we are used to calling psychoanalytic questions. Yet I feel that, just because we are psychoanalysts, we have a desire for greater clarity as to these problems, even where they transcend our immediate clinical, theoretical, and technical concern. We want to understand what light analysis can shed on moral behavior and its motivations; we also want to know what the

[101]

actual or possible relations of our findings are to our personal systems of moral values, and to individual or cultural moral value systems in general.

I have tried to keep some order in presenting to you the different aspects of our subject. This has proved impossible in some instances; the matter is intricate, and repetitions could not always be avoided. I am more embarrassed by the incompleteness and, particularly as to some parts of it, the sketchy character, of this lecture. In regard to what a few might well consider my most regrettable omission—that I did not try to adduce arguments for or against specific moral directions—I fully explained to you why I had to exclude any such attempt from my discussion. I did not avoid this aspect because I am blind to its importance, but because I realize that it has no place in scientific discourse. It belongs in the realm not of science but of ultimate personal positions; no scientific psychology, even if it were perfected beyond what it is today, could take the place of personal responsibility in these matters. But I am sure there were many other questions which, while you listened, obtruded on the thoughts of each one of you and which I failed to answer, which I dealt with only insufficiently or did not touch upon at all.

As to these other questions, I agree with you. I felt the same when I wrote the paper and while I read it now. As to some of them, I may claim that so far, we just do not seem to have the knowledge that would enable us to answer them. May I ask you, then, to accept what I told you as prolegomena to future developments—more explicit and more thorough—rather than as a fully organized whole.

References

I have included in the following list those books and papers which I have quoted or discussed in my lecture. I added out of the considerable literature on this and related subjects the works of some authors who studied different aspects of the problems we dealt with, or the same aspects from different angles. In some instances of the works listed below, the conclusions arrived at are quite contrary to my own views.

Andreas-Salome, L. (1931), *Dank an Freud*. Wien: Psychoanalytischer Verlag.

Binswanger, L. (1956), *Erinnerungen an Sigmund Freud*. Bern: Francke Verlag.

Brierley, M. (1947), Notes on Psycho-analysis and Integrative Living. *International Journal of Psycho-Analysis, 28*:57-105.

Dewey, J. (1922), *Human Nature and Conduct*. New York: Henry Holt.

Fenichel, O. (1945), The Means of Education. *The Psychoanalytic Study of the Child, 1*:281-291. New York: International Universities Press.

Feuer, L. S. (1955), *Psychoanalysis and Ethics*. Springfield, Ill.: Charles C Thomas.

Flugel, J. C. (1945), *Man, Morals and Society*. New York: International Universities Press.

Freud, A. (1935), *Introduction to Psychoanalysis for Teachers and Parents*. New York: Emerson Books.

————(1936), *The Ego and the Mechanisms of Defense*. New York: International Universities Press, 1946.

Freud, S. (1915), Letter to J. J. Putnam. In: *The Life and Work of Sigmund Freud, 2*, by E. Jones. New York: Basic Books, 1955.

————(1923), *The Ego and the Id*. London: Hogarth Press, 1950.

————(1926), *The Problem of Anxiety*. New York: W. W. Norton, 1950.

————(1930), *Civilization and Its Discontents*. London: Hogarth Press, 1950.

————(1932), *New Introductory Lectures on Psychoanalysis*. New York: W. W. Norton, 1933.

————(1936), A Disturbance of Memory on the Acropolis. *Collected Papers, 5*:302-312. London: Hogarth Press, 1950.

Fromm, E. (1947), *Man for Himself*. New York: Rinehart.

Furtmüller, C. (1912), *Psychoanalyse und Ethik*. München: Reinhardt.

Galdston, I., ed. (1955), *Ministry and Medicine in Human Relations*. New York: International Universities Press.

Gewirth, A. (1956), Psychoanalysis and Ethics—Mental or Moral Health? *The Christian Register*.

Hartmann, H. (1927), *Die Grundlagen der Psycho-analyse.* Leipzig: Thieme.

———(1928), Psychoanalyse und Wertproblem. *Imago, 14*:421-440.

———(1933), Psychoanalyse und Weltanschauung. *Psychoanalytische Bewegung, 5*:416-429.

———(1939), Psycho-analysis and the Concept of Health. *International Journal of Psycho-Analysis, 20*:308-321.

———(1939), *Ego Psychology and the Problem of Adaptation.* New York: International Universities Press, 1958.

———(1947), On Rational and Irrational Action. *Psychoanalysis and the Social Sciences, 1*:359-392. New York: International Universities Press.

Hoffer, W. (1945), Psychoanalytic Education. The *Psychoanalytic Study of the Child, 1*:293-308. New York: International Universities Press.

Huxley, J. (1947), In: *Touchstone for Ethics,* by T. H. Huxley and J. Huxley. New York and London: Harper.

Jacobson, E. (1954), The Self and the Object World. *The Psychoanalytic Study of the Child, 9*:75-127. New York: International Universities Press.

Jones, E. (1953-1957), *The Life and Work of Sigmund Freud,* 3 Vols. New York: Basic Books.

Kahler, E. (1957), *The Tower and the Abyss.* New York: George Braziller.

Kaplan, A. (1957), Freud and Modern Philosophy. In: *Freud and the 20th Century,* ed. B. Nelson. New York: Meridian Books.

REFERENCES

Kluckhohn, C. (1951), Values and Value-Orientation in the Theory of Action. In: *Toward a General Theory of Action,* ed. T. Parsons and E. Shils. Cambridge: Harvard University Press.

Kris, E. (1952), *Psychoanalytic Explorations in Art.* New York: International Universities Press.

Lewis, C. J. (1946), *Analysis of Knowledge and Valuation.* La Salle, Ill.: Open Court Publ. Co.

Marcuse, H. (1955), *Eros and Civilization.* Boston: Beacon Press.

Money-Kyrle, R. E. (1952), Psycho-analysis and Ethics. *International Journal of Psycho-Analysis, 33:* 225-234.

————(1955), The Anthropological and the Psychoanalytic Concept of the Norm. *Psychoanalysis and the Social Sciences, 4:*51-60. New York: International Universities Press.

Neumann, E. (1949), *Tiefenpsychologie und neue Ethik.* Zürich: Rascher Verlag.

Nunberg, H. (1932), *Principles of Psychoanalysis.* New York: International Universities Press, 1955.

Odier, C. (1943), *Les deux sources conscientes et inconscientes de la vie morale.* Neuchâtel: Éditions de la Bacconière.

Piaget, J. (1932), *Le jugement moral chez l'enfant.* Paris: Felix Alcan.

Posinsky, S. H. (1958), Instincts, Culture and Science. *Psychoanalytic Quarterly, 37:*1-37.

Reid, J. R. (1955), The Problem of Value in Psychoanalysis. *American Journal of Psychoanalysis, 15:*115-122.

Reider, N. (1950), The Concept of Normality. *Psychoanalytic Quarterly, 19:*43-51.

REFERENCES

Richard, G. (1946), *La psychanalyse et la morale.* Lausanne: Librairie Payot.

Trilling, L. (1955), *Freud and the Crisis of Our Culture.* Boston: Beacon Press.

van den Haag, E. (1959), Psychoanalysis and Its Discontents. In: *Psychoanalysis, Scientific Method, and Philosophy,* ed. S. Hook. New York: New York University Press.

Waddington, C. H., ed. (1942), *Science and Ethics.* London: Allen & Unwin.

Weber, M. (1921), *The Theory of Social and Economical Organization.* New York: Oxford University Press, 1947.

Among works relevant to our topic which I read only after the completion of this essay, I want to mention: Philip Rieff (1959), *Freud: The Mind of the Moralist.* New York: Viking Press; and Fredrick C. Redlich (1959), Die Psychoanalyse und das Wertproblem. *Psyche* (Heidelberg), 13:481-498.

Heinz Hartmann, M.D.

Born in Vienna, 1894. Medical degree at the University of Vienna, 1920. Psychiatric and Neurologic Institute of the University of Vienna 1920-1934. First didactic analysis 1926; second didactic analysis 1934-1936. Member of and Training Analyst at the Psychoanalytic Institutes of Vienna; Paris; New York. Editor *Internationale Zeitschrift für Psychoanalyse* 1932-1941. Editor *The Psychoanalytic Study of the Child* since its first appearance 1945. Director Treatment Center of the New York Psychoanalytic Institute 1948-1951. President, New York Psychoanalytic Society 1952-1954. President, International Psychoanalytic Association, 1951-1957. Honorary President, International Psychoanalytic Association since 1959.

Publications by Dr. Hartmann

1917

(& L. Zila) Über die sogenannte Chiningewöhnung. *Münch. med. Wochschr.*, 64:1597-1598

1918

(& L. Zila) Das Schicksal des Chinins im Organismus. *Arch. exper. Pathol. & Pharmakol.*, 83:221-234

1922

Ein Fall von Depersonalisation. *Ztschr. Neurol. & Psychiat.*, 74:593-601

Zur Frage der Selbstblendung. *Jb. Psychiat. & Neurol.*, 41:171-188

1923

(& P. Schilder) Zur Klinik und Psychologie der Amentia. *Ztschr. Neurol. & Psychiat.*, 92:531-596; also in: *Monatschr. Psychiat. & Neurol.*, 55:321-326, 1924

1924

Ein Beitrag zur Frage der katatonischen Pupillen-starre. *Wien. klin. Wochschr.,* 37:1013-1015

(& S. Betlheim) Über Fehlreaktionen bei der Kor-sakoffschen Psychose. *Arch. Psychiat. & Nervenkr.,* 72:278-286

> English: (condensed) On Parapraxes in the Kor-sakow psychosis. In: *Organization and Pathology of Thought,* ed. & tr. D. Rapaport. New York: Columbia University Press, 1951

Halluzinierte Flächenfarben und Bewegungen. *Monat-schr. Psychiat. & Neurol.,* 56:1-14

1925

Ein Beitrag zur Lehre von den reaktiven Psychosen. *Monatschr. Psychiat. & Neurol.,* 57:89-108

Kokainismus und Homosexualität. *Ztschr. Neurol. & Psychiat.,* 95:79-94; also in: *Dtsch. med. Woch-schr.,* 54:268-270, 1928

(& P. Schilder) Zur Psychologie Schädelverletzter. *Arch. Psychiat. & Nervenkr.,* 75:287-300

Ein weiterer Beitrag zur Selbstblendungsfrage, *Jb. Psychiat. & Neurol.,* 44:31-36

(& P. Schilder) Hypnoseversuche an Paralytikern. *Jb. Psychiat. & Neurol.,* 44:194-202

1927

Zur Frage organische Amnesie und Hypnose. Ver-suche an Korsakoffkranken. *Wien. klin. Woch-schr.,* 40:1507-1508

(& P. Schilder) Körperinneres und Körperschema. *Ztschr. Neurol. & Psychiat.*, 109:666-675

Die Grundlagen der Psychoanalyse. Leipzig: Thieme

1928

(& F. Stumpfl) Ein zwillingspathologischer Beitrag zur Frage: Idiotypus, Paratypus und Neurose. *Wien. med. Wochschr.*, 78:911-915

Psychoanalyse und Wertproblem. *Imago*, 14:421-440

1929

Über genetische Charakterologie, insbesondere über psychoanalytische. *Jb. Charakterol.*, 6:73-96

1930

Abreagieren. Assoziationen. Fausse reconnaissance, déjà vu, déjà éprouvé. Komplexreaktionen. Psychische Energie. Psychoanalyse. Tagträume. Traum. Trieb. Unbewusstes. Verdrängung. [Articles in] *Handwörterbuch für medizinische Psychologie.* Leipzig: Thieme

(& F. Stumpfl) Psychosen bei eineiigen Zwillingen. *Ztschr. Neurol. & Psychiat.*, 123:251-298

Gedächtnis und Lustprinzip. Untersuchungen an Korsakoffkranken. *Ztschr. Neurol. & Psychiat.*, 126: 496-519

1931

(& E. Stengel) Studien zur Psychologie des induzierten Irreseins. *Arch. Psychiat. & Nervenkr.*, 95:584-600

[115]

(& A. Adler) Malariabehandlung einer schwangeren Paralytikerin. *Dtsch. med. Wochschr.*, 57:2018-2019

(& M. Weissman) Zur Decholinbehandlung der Melancholie. *Med. Klin.*, 27:1819-1820

1932

(& E. Stengel) Studien zur Psychologie des induzierten Irreseins. *Jb. Psychiat. & Neurol.*, 48:164-183

Zwillingsforschung in der Psychiatrie. *Wien. klin. Wochschr.*, 45:1592

1933

Psychoanalyse und Weltanschauung. *Psa. Bewegung*, 5:416-429

Der entwicklungspsychologische Gedanke in der Neurosenlehre. *Wien. med. Wochschr.*, 83:971-973

Über Zwillingsforschung in der Psychiatrie. *Wien. med. Wochschr.*, 83:781-785; 809-811

Psychiatrische Zwillingsstudien. *Jb. Psychiat. & Neurol.*, 50:195-242

Ein experimenteller Beitrag zur Psychologie der Zwangsneurose. Über das Behalten erledigter und unerledigter Handlungen. *Jb. Psychiat. & Neurol.*, 50:243-278

(& F. Stumpfl) Ein Beitrag zum Thema: Zwillingsprobleme und Schizophrenie und zur Frage der Vererbung musikalischer Begabung. *Ztschr. Neurol. & Psychiat.*, 143:349-380

[116]

1935

Das Korsakowsche Syndrom. *Wien. klin. Wochschr.*, 48:457-459

Zur Charakterologie erbgleicher Zwillinge. *Jb. Psychiat. & Neurol.*, 52:57-120

1939

Ich-Psychologie und Anpassungsproblem. *Int. Ztschr. Psa.*, 24:62-135

  English: (condensed) Ego Psychology and the Problem of Adaptation. In: *Organization and Pathology of Thought,* ed. & tr. D. Rapaport. New York: Columbia University Press, 1951; see also sub 1958

1942

Psychoanalysis and the Concept of Health. *Int. J. Psa.*, 20:308-321

1943

Psychiatry: Its Relationship to Psychological Schools of Thought. In: *Psychiatry and the War,* ed. F. J. Sladen. Springfield, Ill.: Charles C Thomas

1944

The Psychiatric Work of Paul Schilder. *Psa. Rev.*, 31:287-298

Psychoanalysis and Sociology. In: *Psychoanalysis Today,* ed. S. Lorand. New York: International Universities Press

1945

(& E. Kris) The Genetic Approach in Psychoanalysis. *The Psychoanalytic Study of the Child,* 1:11-30; also in *The Yearbook of Psychoanalysis,* 2:1-22. New York: International Universities Press, 1946
German: Die genetische Betrachtungsweise in der Psychoanalyse. *Psyche* (Heidelberg), 3:1-17, 1949

1946

(& E. Kris, R. M. Loewenstein) Comments on the Formation of Psychic Structure. *The Psychoanalytic Study of the Child,* 2:11-38
Spanish: Comentarios sobre la formación de la estructura psíquica. Rev. Psicoanál., 8:222-248

1947

On Rational and Irrational Action. *Psychoanalysis and the Social Sciences,* 1:359-392. New York: International Universities Press

1948

Comments on the Psychoanalytic Theory of Instinctual Drives. *Psa. Quart.,* 17:368-388

1949

The New York Psychoanalytic Treatment Center. *Bull. Am. Psa. Assn.,* 5:11-13
(& E. Kris, R. M. Loewenstein) Notes on the Theory of Aggression. *The Psychoanalytic Study of the*

Child, 3/4:9-36. New York: International Universities Press

Spanish: Notas sobre la teoría de la agressión. *Rev. Psicoanál.,* 8:402-429

1950

The Application of Psychoanalytic Concepts to Social Science. *Psa. Quart.,* 19:385-392; also in: *The Yearbook of Psychoanalysis,* 7:81-87. New York: International Universities Press, 1951

Psychoanalysis and Developmental Psychology. *The Psychoanalytic Study of the Child,* 5:7-17. New York: International Universities Press

Comments on the Psychoanalytic Theory of the Ego. *The Psychoanalytic Study of the Child,* 5:74-96. New York: International Universities Press

1951

Technical Implications of Ego Psychology. *Psa. Quart.,* 20:31-43

(& E. Kris, R. M. Loewenstein) Some Psychoanalytic Comments on "Culture and Personality." In: *Psychoanalysis and Culture,* ed. G. B. Wilbur & W. Muensterberger. New York: International Universities Press

1952

The Mutual Influences in the Development of Ego and Id. *The Psychoanalytic Study of the Child,* 7:9-30. New York: International Universities Press

1953

(& E. Kris, R. M. Loewenstein) The Function of Theory in Psychoanalysis. In: *Drives, Affects, Behavior,* ed. R. M. Loewenstein. New York: International Universities Press

Contribution to the Metapsychology of Schizophrenia. *The Psychoanalytic Study of the Child,* 8:177-198. New York: International Universities Press

1954

In: Problems of Infantile Neurosis; a Discussion. *The Psychoanalytic Study of the Child,* 9:16-71. New York: International Universities Press

1955

Notes on the Theory of Sublimation. *The Psychoanalytic Study of the Child,* 10:9-29. New York: International Universities Press

1956

Notes on the Reality Principle. *The Psychoanalytic Study of the Child,* 11:31-53. New York: International Universities Press

The Development of the Ego Concept in Freud's Work. *Int. J. Psa.,* 37:425-438

1957

Ernst Kris, 1900-1957. *The Psychoanalytic Study of the Child,* 12:9-15. New York: International Universities Press

PUBLICATIONS BY DR. HARTMANN

1958

Ego Psychology and the Problem of Adaptation [Journal of the American Psychoanalytic Association Monograph No. 1], tr. D. Rapaport. New York: International Universities Press

Comments on the Scientific Aspects of Psychoanalysis. *The Psychoanalytic Study of the Child*, 13:127-146. New York: International Universities Press

1959

Psychoanalysis as a Scientific Theory. In: *Psychoanalysis, Scientific Method, and Philosophy*, ed. S. Hook. New York: New York University Press

THE FREUD ANNIVERSARY LECTURE SERIES
THE NEW YORK PSYCHOANALYTIC INSTITUTE

Previously published volumes

FREUD: MAN AND SCIENTIST
  by *Rudolph M. Loewenstein*

DREAMS AND THE USES OF
  REGRESSION
    by *Bertram D. Lewin*

A GENETIC FIELD THEORY OF EGO
  FORMATION: ITS IMPLICATIONS
  FOR PATHOLOGY
    by *René A. Spitz*